Women Obtaining the Breakthrough: Finding Your Place

Women Obtaining the Breakthrough

Many years ago, I started an online class helping women get to their breakthrough; little did I know that I would have a ministry and coaching business that would do the same. This book is the elaboration of the online class. Many things have been added and adjusted but it still has the same results; finding you while obtaining the breakthrough.

I feel, in our current lives, that we have to do what God says do in His word, with spiritual directions from the teachers and preachers that HE sends. Women Obtaining the Breakthrough will help women from all walks of life get to a point of seeing why GOD keeps them. It a book of encouragement and motivation to move from one level to the next; never will a woman have to deal with rejection without help!

As a minister, teacher, mother and business coach, I have learned that women take the brunt of everything in their lives. Now, I am here to help get you through spiritually and with great expectation that God is meeting you at every level.

Are you ready? Then let's go!

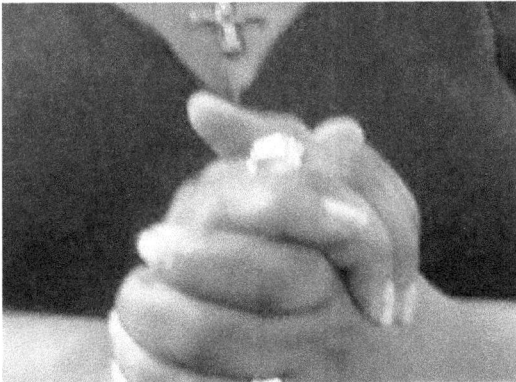

TABLE OF CONTENTS

When the Going gets rough!

We, as women, live a full life. We are moms, wives, business owners and more. Sometimes we feel like we don't get a break, but I want to tell you that when the going gets rough, we can look at scripture that gives us direction.

I remember being on Welfare and trying to pay $300 in rent, $100 in heat and still trying to pay the light bill all while receiving $440 for my child and myself. I thought who lives like this? I had to borrow to buy diapers; borrow to wash clothes; borrow borrow borrow! I was in college with my first child and the going had gotten rough! Determined to get through, I did all I could. I had another child while finishing my Associates Degree in Police Science; I got through, still on Welfare and walking in the grace and favor of God. I remember the poem Still I Rise by Maya Angelou; if God didn't wake me up every morning, my children would have been lost.

During this time of utilizing government benefits, I worked odd jobs to have extra to get the necessities. I even worked in unsafe places for a woman. I didn't realize that I had resources; I didn't realize that I could go far with what I had. During this time, people were concerned with furthering their education, not building businesses. They wanted to start careers. It was ten years and one more child later that I realized I had resources at my fingertips; something that God had instilled in me as a woman to help my family get over.

(If you want to learn how to get off government assistance, you will have to read the information at the end of this book)

Proverbs 31: 13-15 *She finds wool and flax and busily spins it. She is like a merchant's ship, bringing her food from afar. She gets up before dawn to prepare breakfast for her household and plan the day's work for her servant girls.*

This scripture tells us we have the resources to make ends meet. You may not know how to sew, but you might know how to sell! You may not know how to sell, but you are creative in many ways. In the current economy, times are surly rough. The Proverbs 31 woman knows what to do without batting an eyelash or breaking a nail, but where do we start to know that we are that woman?

Women are strong willed creatures. Yet, there are times where the going is too rough, and women will lose their foothold on life. When the bills are due, no food in the fridge, and the children need money for a field trip, a mother will pull her hair out silently.

Proverbs 14:13 *Laughter can conceal a heavy heart, but when the laughter ends, the grief remains.*

Finding ways to pull it all together and never let the family see you sweat is a struggle for all women. Struggle does not discriminate; not by age, gender, race or religion. Look at the lives of some of the famous women in history or in your own friends or family; they have suffered to be where they are today (dead or alive). Women have gone through to get through. What was their motivation? If they didn't have support, what pushed them over the edge for their families and their lives?

Although wives are to submit to their husbands (because they are the head of the house) women are still the innovative strong women as seen in the above verses in Proverbs. When the going gets rough and the husband doesn't have the answer, here are a few things to help get moving and release you from the struggle:

- Start your day with prayer.
- Read your bible daily.
- Write down your goals and aspirations.
- Set a schedule/time line to obtain those goals
- Start to eliminate those things that cause negative reactions/responses in your home.
- Talk to your husband and children about the changes

you are trying to make for a better life.

- ASK, SEEK, KNOCK--you cannot do everything alone,
  - delegate home projects to the children or your husband.

Take time to evaluate your current circumstances and understand it is okay to be weak. Understand it is okay to say I need a way out and I need it now! It's okay to have all the feelings you have just don't sin in those feelings. Its okay to cry sometimes, just don't let the spirit of depression over take you.

Assignment:

Study Proverbs 31:10-31 and write down what the spirit has shown you.

Find 3 scriptures that illuminate YOU and your life right now.

Write a prayer asking God to help you get to your breakthrough.

_____

_____
_____
_____
_____

Keep Moving

In the first chapter I asked you to evaluate yourself. Using the scriptures provided and finding three of your own, you should have come up with an honest viewpoint of who and where you are now in your life.

The purpose of the scriptural evaluation is to help you see that you may not be who God wants you to be and where you are going in the rough times might not be HIS plan of action. Now that you have done your evaluation, keep moving!

We have to be honest with ourselves. As women, we are so strong willed that, sometimes, we want to say that we have it all together, but I remember a time when I thought I was losing my mind trying to do it all. God doesn't want us to lose our minds. He wants us to lean on Him. So in the scriptures YOU found for you, be honest and know who you are and who you are not. Now as I said, keep moving, don't let any of it get you down.

GOD CAN HEAR

The purpose of the breakthrough is to keep moving despite the trials and the tribulations. I have written this chapter in two sections, God can hear and Eliminate the obstacles, to show you how allowing God to move those things out of your life that are hindering your spiritual success will help you see the breakthrough in the little things everyday. It is about acknowledging that you are not perfect and you cannot do it without HIS strength. So, let's get started.

In order to pull on the strength from the Lord you have to realize God can hear. He can hear when you cry out about the situation and He can hear you when you thank Him in the midst of the situation. Use your voice; turn yourself into your heart and cry out to the Father in Heaven.

1 Peter 4:11 *If anyone speaks, he should do it as one speaking the very words of God. If anyone serves, he should do it with the strength God provides, so that in all things God may be praised through Jesus Christ. To him be the glory and the power fore ever and ever. Amen.*

Psalm 118:5-6 *In my anguish I cried to the Lord, and he answered by setting me free. The Lord is with me; I will not be afraid. What can man do to me?*

Psalm 118:29 *Give thanks to the Lord, for his good; his love endures forever.*

Psalm 121:2 *My help comes from the Lord, the Maker of heaven and earth.*

I have been taught to pray the scriptures back to God; He honors HIS word. So, while crying out to HIM and pulling on HIS strength, say the scriptures back to HIM. He can hear!

ELIMINATE THE OBSTACLES

The purpose of asking, seeking and knocking, according to Matt. Chap. 7:7-8, is to get direction from God on what HE wants for you. Most times there are obstacles that are in our way of success and prosperity. These obstacles can come in many forms:

- People
- Material Things
- Money(finances)

- Self

If any of these things are tripping you over in life, it is time for elimination! Time to ask God to help you get rid of these obstacles!

People-- people that do not have a spiritual connection cannot help you effectively in getting your breakthrough. NOTE: Even if they have a connection, you will have to use spiritual discernment to know their advice is for you. This is where prayer and relationship with GOD comes in. If you don't have a relationship with your Father, you won't be able to test the spirit by the spirit.

Material Things-- Matt. 6: 19-21 *Do not store up for yourselves treasures on earth, where moth and rust destroy, and where thieves break in and steal. But store up for your selves treasures in heaven,* *where moth and rust do not destroy, and where thieves do not break in and steal. For where your treasure is, there your heart will be also.* Material possessions are not important to your salvation. This means, while you are trying to have the best everything you are not thinking about your walk with God or how much worry you are putting on material things. I regret buying my children everything I could buy when they were young, even if it wasn't what they wanted. Sometimes you have to decide not to spend foolishly or haphazardly if it will affect your home life or future success. Material things can catch fire, get stolen, or just stop working!

Money-- Ecc. 5: 10 *Whoever loves money never has money enough; whoever loves wealth is never satisfied with his income.* Money is the root of all evil when you use it the wrong way. You can pay your tithes, pay your mortgage, etc., but when you gamble with it or spend it foolishly, you are going to reap exactly what you sow! I'm a victim of spending foolishly and my marriage suffered. It took a lot of reflection on my part to get us back on track.

Self-- if you are not humble and are prideful you are defeating the purpose of any type of breakthrough in your life. Asking God to eliminate you is the best prayer request possible. Women have the habit of putting themselves first in their lives without caring what the outcome will be. (If you did the assignment from the first module, reading Proverbs 31, you will understand that the woman God made and has filled with the spirit is not selfish and prideful.) Women are to put God first, then Husband (if married), then children, career/business, and then self. Prov. 31:30 *Charm is deceptive, and beauty is fleeting; but a woman who fears the Lord is to be praised.* Get yourself out of the way.

Your motivation right now is to keep moving. Do not let the people of the world see you sweat; praise God in the midst of your trials and triumphs! Allow Him to eliminate the things in your life that are hindering your spiritual success.

Assignment

You must start somewhere to keep moving. If you are struggling to understand how to keep moving this week's assignment will help:

Write a prayer asking God to give you strength.

_____

_____

_____

_____

_____

Study Psalm 119: 125 Find where you are NOT in this scripture and study it often. (I suggest you use all resources available to you)

The Power of Words (Your Tongue)

What did you find out about yourself in Psalm 119:125?The assignments in the previous chapters asked you to look at who you are. **Psalm 119: 125** says *I am your servant; give me discernment that I may understand your statutes.*

What are the statutes and what do they say? Where are you being led in the statutes? What are you doing to learn what they are?

Obtaining the breakthrough is not about you being wrong, it is about finding you and doing what is right. The bible was written as instructions to help you get by in those times where it seems the sun will not come up for you and the night is long. Let me tell you that not only does the sun shine on the just and the unjust the SON shines as well. Look at GOD!

WHERE IS YOUR HEART?

Below are a few scriptures involving your heart. Wherever your heart is, that is where your mind will be. Some of the breakthrough is going to come from changing your heart and directing your mind. We will go into great detail about the tongue and being humble, but let's first look at God's word on the heart.

Exodus 25:2 *Tell the Israelites to bring me an offering. You are to receive the offering for me from each man whose heart prompts him to give.*

2 Chronicles 17:6 *His heart was devoted to the ways of the Lord; furthermore, he removed the high* *places and the Asherah poles from Judah.*

Psalm 14:1 *The fool says in his heart, "There is no God." They are corrupt, their deeds are vile; there is no one who does good.*

Ecclesiastes 11:10 *So then, banish anxiety from your heart and cast off the troubles of your body, for youth and vigor are meaningless.*

Acts 1:24 and 25 *Then they prayed, Lord, you know everyone's heart. Show us which of these two you have chosen to take over this apostolic ministry, which Judas left to go where be belongs.*
What is in your heart comes out of your mouth and can be either bring life or death. Your heart is important to a full life for you and your descendants.

You literally have to put your emotions (your heart) in check on some of the things of your life. You want to have a clean heart before God in all that you do. So, like in the last chapter, you have to move YOU out of the way and walk in complete love. I know that may be hard; people have hurt you and the pain still lingers. The only way God can heal you is if you forgive the ones that hurt you and get your heart right.

POWER OF WORDS (BASICALLY YOUR TONGUE)

Let us make this process easier by finding statutes or scripture that pertain to you. This chapter is about the power of words; your words. What scripture tells you, there is extreme power behind your words whether good or bad? What does scripture tell you to do? The power of the tongue is strong and you should take a minute to apply the word to your mind to keep your tongue on track.

Psalm 5:9 *Not a word from their mouth can be trusted; their heart is filled with destruction. Their throat is an open grave; with their tongue they speak deceit.*

Psalm 34:13 *Keep your tongue from evil and your lips from speaking lies.*
Psalm 37:30 *The mouth of the righteous man utters wisdom, and his tongue speaks what is just.*

Proverbs 6: 16 and 17: *There are six things that Lord hates, seven that are detestable to him; haughty eyes, a lying tongue...*

Proverbs 10:19 and 20: *When words are many, sin is not absent, but he who holds his tongue is wise. The tongue of the righteous is* *choice silver, but the heart of the wicked is of little value.*

Proverbs 21:23 *He who guards his mouth and his tongue keeps himself from calamity.*
.

The above scripture give you instruction while also providing the result if you do not adhere to what is read. As in Deuteronomy Chapter 28, where you have the blessings for obedience and the curses for obedience; these are instructions and you have to know them. Keep them on your tongue and in your heart. You do not want your tongue to put your salvation in jeopardy.

Have you noticed that if you are slow to speak, the pain eases? You will not say anything you cannot take back. It is hard to "relearn" your scripture and apply it to your life, but take time to do it everyday. Ask the Lord to change your heart and your mind in order for your tongue to illuminate what is in both!

HUMBLE YOURSELF

You are going to have many trials where you may have to settle for what seems less for you. This is going to be a time of humbling.

Humble means (dictionary.com) not proud or arrogant; modest courteously respectful to make meek

Christians are practicing being humble everyday, while they are also practicing changing their tongue. If you have always been a woman who is strong willed, or an out spoken go getter, you may find it difficult to humble yourself. You are who YOU are for a reason, but
as I stated before, you may not be where GOD wants you be. Use this chapter to focus on your tongue and

how it is being affected by your heart and your mind. If this may seem a slight bit in reverse it is not. You started this book because you know (mind) and feel (heart) that you need a breakthrough for something in your life. You will have to put your heart in check for your tongue to be on track.

God wakes you up everyday to give you a chance to do everything differently and choose HIM to guide you!

Assignment:

Study scriptures on heart and tongue. You may have to go to your concordance or use online resources.

Don't Give Up: Working it out biblically

I pray this book is helping you get started to obtain your breakthrough! It's a slow process. Nothing changes overnight, but God is able to get you through if you lean on HIM!

So, we are not at NOT giving up. Have you ever been in a position where you were just too tired to keep going and running this race? Giving has looked like a great option hasn't it?

I had some issues in my life where I just wanted to sit down and sleep. I didn't want to work on what God had for me; I didn't want to work in ministry or have a business. I just wanted to give up on all that was waiting for me and my family; for

29

our future. God put in my spirit that giving up was not an option.

Giving up is something that people do because it is very easy. These are people that are not rooted in the Lord. People that do not have a spiritual connection! Giving up is not an option. If you are married and you are not feeling 100% adequate in your relationship, divorce (a form of giving up) is not an option. If you are a parent of a teenager that does not, will not listen to you, you cannot walk away (another form of giving up). In laymen's terms, giving up is a cop out to dealing with the circumstances. This book is about breakthrough and finding your place spiritually, which means you do not have a choice in the matter. If you give up the spirit may snap you back into place and you will feel that you are at a point of starting everything all over!

What do you do? Start with the spiritual basics of not giving up.

1. Prayer
    a. Yes, we may have talked about this previously, but the help is in the power of saying you NEED help. Pray about

    it. Talk to your Father in heaven as if He is sitting next to you listening intently. You may have cry a little or even a lot but pray about.
    b. Ask the Lord to show you where you have failed. Sometimes we are the problem, ladies. Most times we do not know when to sit back and humble ourselves and HUSH! You will need the spirit to come in and show you where

you have failed and where you have been wrong.

2. Study Scripture and Apply it
   a. It is important to get in your word, study the scripture and apply it. This can not be repeated enough. It can only be worked out by you. You may not be the author or finisher of your life, but you are the one to choose to do the right things to get to that breakthrough.
   b. The best way to study the scripture and applying to the areas of your life that may be hindering you, is to use your concordance (in the back of your bibles) and find the word or issues that best pertain to you. Find words like,

woman or women, heart, hurt, love, submission, obedience. Find words that will help YOU individually.

3. Participate in continuous fellowship
   a. Make sure you attend Sunday service and bible study. It will help you get an understanding of your walk. It will teach you how to keep an active conversation with God. (continuous prayer) Bible study is essential, because it allows you to ask questions. This is a form of staying active in obtaining your breakthrough; you are obtaining wisdom that keeps you from giving up.

Giving up is not an option. The breakthrough is obtained through the means of practice and persistence. You will develop patience in all those around you as you seek the Lord continuously through various means.

Where are you now?

Okay, so here we are at the end of the book. Have you challenged yourself to get through to your breakthrough? Have you seen that in many different facets of your life?

The information you have obtained here you might have heard before in church or in your individual ministries. It is important to "talk" to one another to find out what else should be added to the wealth of information you need now.

So, ladies, where are you now?

What is the spirit putting inside of you about your life?

Have you seen some change, even the size of a mustard seed?

Have you felt the Lord's pulling on your life? Pulling on the plan he has for you and not the plan you have for yourself?

I hope you will refer to this book daily, monthly, and sometimes, annually to keep obtaining the breakthrough in your life.

God bless!

Dana M. Neal

ABOUT THE AUTHOR

Wife, Mother, and CEO (Christian Encouragement Officer), Mrs. Dana Neal works hard to establish business and personal connections that will last a life time. As a motivational speaker and writer, Mrs. Neal is ready to put light into your life that only comes from above! When the joy of life is interrupted by negative situations, there becomes a need for motivation and encouragement. Dana has been writing poetry and short stories since she was a teen; returning to her first loves of writing and speaking, Mrs. Neal has written a variety of books on self-help and how-to, poetry and spiritual encouragement! Psalm 45:1 My heart is overflowing with a good theme; I recite my composition concerning the King; My tongue is the pen of a ready writer.

OTHER RESOURCES:

Visit www.baduniversity.com for information regarding the following

No More Food stamps

On/offline class for persons attempting to get off of government assistant and start their own business or create residual income while working;

Triple D's: Divas, Diamonds, and Discounts (tips tricks and, couponing)